MW01283268

The Four Seasons of my Primitive Life

The Four Seasons of my Primitive Life

An Inspirational Journey

GAIL REEDER

gatekeeper press™
Columbus, Ohio

The views and opinions expressed in this book are solely those of the author and do not reflect the views or opinions of Gatekeeper Press. Gatekeeper Press is not to be held responsible for and expressly disclaims responsibility of the content herein.

The Four Seasons of my Primitive Life: An Inspirational Journey

Published by Gatekeeper Press
2167 Stringtown Rd, Suite 109
Columbus, OH 43123-2989
www.GatekeeperPress.com

Copyright © 2022 by Gail Reeder

All rights reserved. Neither this book, nor any parts within it may be sold or reproduced in any form or by any electronic or mechanical means, including information storage and retrieval systems without permission in writing from the author. The only exception is by a reviewer, who may quote short excerpts in a review.

Library of Congress Control Number: t/k

ISBN (paperback): 9781662902581

Dedication

I dedicate this book to my loyal friend, James Brown. On a Saturday afternoon in 1996, he invited Larry and I into his home. We had never met James but his kindness and generosity were displayed that day as he allowed us to tour his beautiful Saltbox home. We were in search of design ideas for our own Saltbox. We became lifelong friends from that day forward. James is an antique dealer and he was always on the lookout for a treasure that we would love to place in our new home. Many of my most beloved  antiques stand proudly in my home today because of this dear friend. James built several of my hanging cupboards and was always willing to lend a helping hand. He actually helped us move into our Saltbox when it was completed. In turn, he enjoyed a few country meals at our table with my family.

To you, James Brown, this dedication represents the value I place on our friendship.

Welcome to my Primitive Home

Fall table scape

Gail Reeder

Spring table scape

Gail Reeder

Summer table scape

Gail Reeder

Christmas table scape

Bill Reeder

Gail Reeder

Foreword

Autumn is a time to slow down. To enjoy the glory of the changing colors and cooler temperatures. My hope, as you read my book, is to sense all four seasons, and to realize that no matter what season of life that you are in, embrace it and be thankful.

May He grant you your hearts desire and fullfill all your plans.

Psalms 20:4

Table of Contents

Bittersweet

It is no secret that Fall is my favorite time of the year. I feel fresh and renewed as the crisp air blows against my face. The colors of the season create a glorious masterpiece in the distance. Snuggled by the fire with a plaid blanket and a pumpkin spice latte' is my happy place. I feel excitement as I bring down totes from the attic to start decorating. I bring the colors of the season into my home with the use of bittersweet, pumpkins, gourds, and fall foliage. I create

a table scape in the kitchen and dining room to boast the season. (How to instructions on page 18). I burn candles with the spicy fragrance of cinnamon and cloves. When you walk in my door the very season wraps you in its arms.

As I think of how my decorating style has evolved over the years, it is a comedy of errors. In my early years of marriage, money was tight and decorating was sparse. A few wood-carved pumpkins and spooky cats from the local craft fair was the flavor of the day. In a few years the money wasn't quite as tight and I upgraded to authentic pumpkins. I have to laugh as I am writing this because I truly thought this décor was just beautiful at the time. And why not? It blended beautifully with my oak furniture, ruffled curtains and my country blue sofa.

In November 1984 my favorite season took a bitter turn for the worse. My husband and the father of my three-year old little girl, Amy, was killed in a tragic and unexpected traffic accident. My world was turned upside down.

It was a cold and rainy Sunday. Amy and I had gone to church as usual on Sunday morning. Dennis did not join us that particular day. He had kissed us goodbye with the assurance that he would attend my niece's birthday party that afternoon. Amy and I arrived at church and had settled into our seats after the usual handshakes and well-wishes typical of a country church. As the congregation bowed their heads for the opening prayer, the creaking sound of the double doors opening drew everyone's attention. There in the frame of the doorway stood a rain-soaked Coroner with a look of desperation on his face. As he scanned the room with his eyes, a cold silence blanketed the sanctuary. The entire congregation knew that the Coroner was about to share devastating news that would change someone's life forever. With every pew that he passed there was a sigh of relief. As he walked closer and closer to the pew where Amy and I were sitting I prayed, dear God don't let it be me. He sat down on our pew and scooted across the seat close to me. He took my hand and said we need to go outside. I felt my heart sink to my feet. I was overpowered with every emotion imaginable. I took Amy's hand and we followed him outside to the covered porch. Cold rain blew in around us. Every inch of my body shivered. He placed his hands on my shoulders and there in that moment my world crumbled right beneath me. Dennis had been in a fatal traffic accident. The moments after that devastating news are a blur to me. I am convinced that shock is God's way of numbing your brain while you come to grips with tragic news.

Dennis and I had built a new home on his parent's farm. We spent endless weekends painting, staining, and hanging wallpaper to save labor cost. The new house was adorned with the Primitive Style. Well, what I thought at the time was Primitive Style. Country blue and oatmeal plaid wallpaper and border with mason jars and pip berries in the kitchen. The round oak table looked stunning with the wallpaper as a backdrop. I used the same color scheme throughout the house. I was just beginning to get the Primitive fever as I decided store bought furniture wasn't going to suffice. Still on a tight budget, I began to scour flea markets and auctions where I purchased my first Primitive piece in the year 1978. The antique pie safe, which (shown here) stands proudly in my guest room to this day. I remember Dennis said, "You actually paid money for this?" He did not have the fever. (His passion was training and showing quarter horses in his spare time, aside from working as a lineman for Tri County Electric). I was in search of an iron bed, and a dresser that I could paint and apply antique finish

to look old and worn. I found the iron bed first and started the refinishing challenge in the garage. Sanding off rust to acquire a smooth enough finish to paint. I painted the bed country blue, distressed it a bit and added an antique finish. And there it was, my masterpiece. Or at least, I thought it was my masterpiece. I then found an antique dresser for a reasonable price of which I painted and antiqued in the same finish. My spare change was depleted by this point so a night stand would have to be added later. As it turned out I was given a round fiber board table (remember those) by a dear friend. This will work just fine, I thought, as I sewed a calico table cloth to drape over it. My lamp was an electrified oil lamp with a blue paper shade boasting a cutout stencil of hearts. My dear mother in law gifted Amy a handmade Dutch doll quilt that I used as a bedspread. This would be Amy's room in our new home. The anticipation engulfed me as we approached moving day. We moved into our new home on Labor Day weekend. He was killed on November 18th. We had barely had time to unpack our belongings. Needless to say, the excitement of our new home vanished and the location was going to be quite awkward for Amy and I to continue our life without him.

The Coldest Winter

Amy and I slept together in the Primitive room I had designed for her. I couldn't bear to sleep alone in a strange house with the cold black space that surrounded me. It was a rough winter with much snow and travel to and from work was difficult. Dennis had always driven me to work on snowy days. To tackle that alone was terrifying. It was a bitter cold night with snow piling up on the window ledge outside. It was that night with tears in her eyes, Amy asked me where did her daddy go. Why doesn't he ever come home anymore? How could I explain this desperate infinity that was our future? It was that night that I decided we had to move. We had to be close to work and family. We had to be where there were street lights and some sound of life outside the dark windows. As I lay there with her in my arms, a situation came to mind of the day that the string on her helium balloon had broken and the balloon floated into space. Into to the blue space above and eventually was completely out of sight. I asked Amy if she remembered that day. She said she did and I explained that is where her daddy is now. He floated into the heavens much like her balloon to be with God and all of his angels. That her daddy will always be with her in spirit and he will always love her. That seemed to satisfy her innocent and confused little mind. She never asked again where her daddy was.

Amy and I had somehow managed to live there for a year. It seemed like an eternity. Dennis' parents approached me about buying our house. They knew how lonely and displaced I felt. They lived in a small country home behind us and were more than willing to upgrade to the new home situated right there on their farm. It was a good situation for both of us. I started planning my second new home and looking for a place to build it. *God is always ahead of our plans*. A lot across the street from my sister and brother in law was available. I bought the lot and contracted with the same builder to start a new home identical to the one he had just built for us. This seemed to be the most reasonable thing to do since I loved the plan of my existing home and the process would be much simpler. He immediately started the construction.

I had an incurable case of Primitive fever by this time. I incorporated wood floors and a more primitive color scheme. I used a country red and navy color scheme, no wallpaper and linen white walls. From my study of Primitive Magazines, I had realized that furniture popped against lighter walls. And a wood floor was a must. I purchased a Johnston's Benchworks sofa and two wing back chairs in navy lovers knot fabric and navy petal fabric respectively. I also purchased a beautiful early cupboard, and had a pencil post bed custom built. Yes, I was beginning to find the true "look". But I wasn't there yet. I loaded the shelves of that early cupboard with wooden craft pieces, tin stars and pip berries. An Americana throw draped proudly over my sofa completed the décor. My goodness, obviously I was still on the wrong track. I continued to study the Primitive Magazines as if I were preparing for a Bar Exam. There were still antique oak pieces scattered throughout. And those ruffled curtains found their way back on my windows in the new home. Washed and starched they hung like billowy ivory clouds.

Amy and I felt more secure here close to family. But the emptiness of losing Dennis was still ever present even in new surroundings. I believe you never recover from the loss of a spouse. It is akin to losing an appendage. You can survive but everything changes. Down to the most minute detail.

Spring Forward

It was the Spring of 1985 when our despondent situation was about to change. Amy and I were in the Mall shopping. I remember watching couples pushing their babies in strollers, holding hands and laughing. Why was I trapped in this glass box of grief with no exit? My very existence was suffocating. I went through the motions of daily activities with no purpose. Aside from being the best single mother I could for Amy. I prayed that God would send us a good Christian man to loves us and take care of us. Believe me when I say that *God is always a few steps ahead of our plans.* Straight ahead I saw a letter carrier. He was delivering mail to all the stores. I remember thinking that must be a pleasant occupation. Inside, out of the weather. Visiting with the proprietors every day. I would learn later that this only took an hour of his day. The remaining seven hours included an eight-mile walking route in the sun, rain, sleet, and snow. Whatever the weather, the mail must be delivered, right?

As we walked closer, I recognized him. It was Larry Reeder, an old flame that I had dated a couple of times in high school. I had not seen him for many years. We had a nice chat and caught up on our thirteen years apart. He offered his condolences for the loss of my husband. We went our separate ways and I assumed that would be the end of that.

Three weeks later, Larry called. Much to my surprise, he invited Amy and myself to a church picnic. We had other plans so that was not going to happen. A few weeks passed and he called again with another invitation to take our girls to Chucky Cheese. I accepted the invitation and the rest is history. We were married in October 1986. He was a kind hearted man and a good father to his daughters, Renee and Amy. He never made a difference in the two. Our happiness was his top priority.

He was in the early stages of designing and building a log cabin when we met. He put that dream on hold and moved in with Amy and I when we got married.

He too had an apparent love of Primitive décor. We settled into this ranch style home and lived there for twelve years. The neighborhood was friendly and safe. Our girls rode their bikes to and from their friend's homes. The country club joined the subdivision for easy access to the pool during summer break.

I was constantly farming out and selling oak pieces to be replaced with early 18th and 19th century pieces. I soon learned that the crafty displays were not the "look" I craved so desperately. Yard sales and drop offs at the Good Will took care of all that fad. I was beginning to learn that true authentic antiques, as shown here, were the "look".

Larry and I loved to go antiquing together. Almost every vacation and holiday we would set out for our next adventure. He was drawn to crocks, while I was drawn to wooden pieces. Early cupboards, firkins, dough bowls, cutting boards, etc. Every occasion that warranted a gift from Larry or my family allowed me to mark off a piece from my wish list. I started collecting redware, pewter, baskets, old coverlets and quilts. This was a slow and grueling process as my Virgo personality needed immediate results. However, money is always a factor so I found patience from somewhere deep inside. I knew that someday I would have the "look" for which I studied relentlessly.

In 1995 Larry and I purchased the most substantial antique in our collection. An 1800's log house. We hired Amish to disassemble the log house and number each log for future use. We saved every salvageable piece of wood to be used soon in our latest venture. To build an authentic Saltbox home. I started a scrapbook of period decorating ideas from magazines, pictures of the Saltbox homes we visited, period lighting and hardware. My precious daddy who was a retired contractor built my kitchen and dining room tables from some of the salvaged poplar lumber. These two tables are priceless. They are in my current home.

Soon after the deconstruction of the log house we put the ranch style home on the market and it sold relatively fast. Where would we live during the construction of our Saltbox? Once again, *God is always a few steps ahead of our plans.* Dennis' mother had been left alone. Her husband and Amy's grandfather had suffered a massive heart attack which took his life soon after they moved into their new home. She invited us to live with her during the construction. What

a turn of events. Here we were living in my previous home with my previous mother-in-law. After all, she could spend quality time with her granddaughter and help us out in the meantime. How noble of her to invite my new husband into her home. We stored all of our furniture and moved in with her for several months.

Finally, the Saltbox home was finished. We used salvaged items from the log house everywhere possible. Including the mantle, poplar beams and wood flooring used as our countertops in the kitchen and baths. The outside of the Saltbox was covered with western cedar siding that we stained colonial blue. With nine over nine windows, colonial red trim around window and doors this was our dream come true. Situated in a two-acre woods that screamed put a Saltbox right here. We spent seventeen years as a family together is this home. Adding period pieces and smalls along the way. Larry and I agreed that this home had its own personality. It literally wrapped its arms around us with love. Our girls left for college and the empty nest syndrome would be cured by travel and our next antiquing adventure.

August 2012 another dream came true. Our home was to be featured in the Fall 2013 issue of A Primitive Place Magazine. When I received the call from the editor earlier that year, I told her that this was the grand finale of our lives. We had collected our entire married lives. To be featured in the magazine was absolutely the grandest compliment imaginable.

A Summer To Remember

Larry spent that summer trimming shrubs, painting doors and picket fences. Cleaning windows and seeding the yard to make sure that our Saltbox was an immaculate showplace for the upcoming photo shoot. He took so much pride in our home inside and out. One afternoon that summer he came home from the farm with a weakness on his right side and a bit of slurred speech. I feared that he'd had a mild stroke. The doctor visit and test proved that to be true.  He was put on an aspirin a day and returned to work after a few weeks. He appeared to have completely recovered. He was scheduled to retire from the United States Postal service in January of the coming year. I had already retired from US Bank. He was so excited about the next chapter of our lives. We planned to travel, continue our passion for antiques and road trips to find the next treasure.

January finally arrived and Larry retired. We started making plans to add a log addition to our Saltbox that would serve as a family room. Our family was growing with the bonus of two son in laws and four grandchildren. However, our plans were abruptly dismantled. February 9th Larry suffered a major stoke. A brain bleed that would take his life in fourteen heartbreaking days. He was on life support with tubes in almost every orifice. Clinging to life by a thin thread. On February 23rd he drew his last breath. He would never see our home in A

Primitive Place Magazine. He would never travel and he would never find that next treasure on our road trips. He would never see his grandchildren grow up. Again, I became a widow. Alone and stricken with grief. This home was too much to attend to alone. This two-acre lot was too large to keep up. What to do now? How do I possibly start over again? Why was this happening to me, AGAIN. So many unanswered questions flooded my exhausted mind.

God is always a step ahead of our plans. Renee and her husband Jake needed more room with a growing family. I needed less room. When Renee offered to buy the Saltbox, I said yes. Larry would be pleased that his daughter and family would live in our dream home. They were willing to let me live in the Saltbox until my new home was finished. What a blessing.

I somehow found the strength to focus on this move rather than the grief that controlled my every breath. I realized it was something that I had to do. I had no choice.

I started the fourth building process soon after. I knew I needed a one-story home and a small yard with less upkeep. I found a lot available in a nearby subdivision and purchased it. I drew my house plan with every detail suited to my furniture. Every corner and nook had a purpose. I used heart pine plank floors with tongue oil finish. I chose Almond Cream walls, Sautéed Mushroom and Kiln Red as trim colors. The mantle was a replica of the original mantle from the log home. I used simple trim and shaker style cabinetry. Ceilings were smooth with no popcorn coating. I chose period lighting throughout. The outside was a colonial style with Hardy Board Siding painted the color Curlew. Brick porches and columns finished the primitive/colonial look. The outside wasn't as Primitive as I would have liked. However, there were restrictions in the subdivision. Each new home was required to compliment the exterior and style of

the existing homes and approved by a building committee. Therefore, a colonial style exterior was my closest option.

I have currently lived in this home for six years. I am very pleased with the neighborhood and pleased with my home as well. It is near both daughters and the grandchildren visit frequently. This home was featured in A Primitive Place Magazine in the Fall issue 2018 and the December 2019 issue of Early American Life Magazine. I still cannot believe that the purchase of that first pie safe in 1978 led to a home that is worthy of a Magazine. I still have a passion for Primitive. However, I buy much less and enjoy what I have. I am sometimes in awe when I see how far I have progressed in my decorating style since my first home. Following years of study my advice would be this. Light walls, period color trim, wood and/or brick floors, 18th century cupboards, period

fabric on sofa and chairs, period style beds, braided or antique oriental rugs, collections displayed "in like kind" inside cupboards (i.e. coverlets, baskets, redware, pewter, yellow ware, old quilts). I finally, after forty years, have the "look". Through it all **I never let go of my vision**.

As seasons change in our lives, we must change with them. We must accept God's plan and ask for guidance and strength. And with each new season, be thankful. May God bless you on your Primitive journey. Have patience **and never let go of your vision.**

You may also visit my home on:
Anne Clay's Primitive Home YouTube channel
and Judy Condon's book, Crisp Days of Autumn (August 2021 issue)

This chapter includes ideas and some of my personal decorating opinions. These opinions are not based on any form of professional skills or education. They are my own ideas base on years of studying the Primitive Style.

Designing A Table Scape

As with any construction start with a foundation. Begin your grouping with a cutting board or a table runner, even a piece of homespun fabric. Any flat surface from which you can build upon. Decide at this point the color scheme of the grouping. A seasonal color palate that compliments the room. Use different textures in your design. For example, a fabric heart, a stoneware crock, and a wooden pantry box. Add different heights by adding florals or greenery to the crock, and a candle atop the pantry box. Place seasonal fruit, pumpkins, pinecones, etc. in the basket. I like to clip a piece of the floral or greenery to tuck beside the candle and/or inside the basket. This brings the grouping together.

This is an example of how to fashion a table scape. Of course, you may tweak it to your own personal taste. Shown here is a gathering I arranged for the Fourth of July.

Shown here are two of my Christmas decorating ideas.

very Primitive lover collects things. Whether it be baskets, crocks, pantry boxes, firkins, coverlets, we all have collections. I have found that collections look best when displayed together. If you have five crocks and they are scattered here and there, they aren't really noticed. However, if you bring them all together inside an early cupboard, they become a focal point in the room. This applies to any other collection you might have. Adding a quilt or coverlet folded and draped over the door also adds interest. Group game boards together on one wall, place firkins together on a bucket bench or stack them in a graduating fashion.

Place red ware in a cupboard or on a plate shelf on the wall. Same goes for pewter. Group samplers together on a wall. You will begin to see that grouping trumps scattered all day long. If you lack enough of one item to be considered a "collection", focus on shopping for more of that particular item until you can create a grouping.

If you are just beginning your Primitive journey, my advice would be to start in one room. Choose the Primitive style that you love. Whether it be rustic, or a cleaner Colonial/Primitive look. A total remodel is too overwhelming. Maybe start in the living room. Buy large pieces first, then fill in with smalls and collections. **It is a marathon not a sprint.** Use resources to find the look you love and study

that look. Create a folder and load it with photos of the style you love. Let that be your guide when purchasing new pieces.

In closing, I would offer this advice. Primitive decorating is a passion. Once you get the fever, there is no cure. Make your home your own. Your home should be a place of refuge. A place you love to spend time. And foremost don't be discouraged. After forty years and many devastating obstacles I have arrived at my "Primitive Home". Where I will be grateful for **memories** and embrace the…….

"THE FOUR SEASONS OF MY PRIMITIVE LIFE"

MAY GOD BLESS YOUR JOURNEY

Dixie Reeder

A Primitive Place,
P. O. Box 197, Forman, ND 58032
www.aprimitiveplace.org

Early American Life,
P. O. Box 221230, Shaker Heights, OH 44122
earlyamericanlife.com

CPSIA information can be obtained
at www.ICGtesting.com
Printed in the USA
BVHW010542080223
658059BV00024B/1143